EGYPTIAN LIFE

BY

JOHN GUY

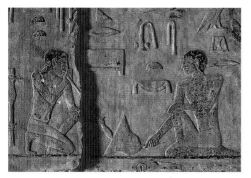

Who were the Ancient Egyptians?

FIRST INDUSTRY

The technique of extracting metal ores from rock was developed in about 4500 BC in both Egypt and Sumeria, which enabled more durable tools and weapons to be made. The metal workers shown here are smelting copper.

Sometime around 5000 BC, mankind organised himself into city-states, the first true civilizations. The process appears to have occurred simultaneously, but quite independently, at different sites across the world. What caused this change in man's basic character from a nomadic to a settled existence we shall probably never know. Nor the precise date it occurred. All we do know is based upon physical remains excavated so far; other sites, older still perhaps, may still await discovery. All of these early civilizations were centred on major river valleys: the Yellow River in China; the Indus River in India; the Tigris-Euphrates in the Middle East and the Nile in Egypt. The Egyptian civilization, although probably not the oldest, grew to become, perhaps, the greatest of these ancient cultures.

THE POTTER'S ART

The Egyptians invented the potter's wheel, sometime around 4000 BC. Before that, pots were fashioned by hand pressing wet clay into shapes and leaving to dry.

THE BEGINNINGS OF FARMING

At about the same time as the founding of the first civilizations (c.5000 BC) mankind also developed the art of cultivating crops. The annual flooding of the river valleys where these first civilizations were established deposited a rich silt on the surrounding land; as happened with the Nile allowing the early Egyptians to cultivate their valley.

Egyptian Empire

Area of Egyptian influence

A KINGDOM UNITED

Originally, Egypt was divided into two kingdoms, Upper and Lower Egypt. They were united under Pharaoh Menes in c.3100 BC, who founded the I dynasty. The period known as the Old Kingdom lasted from the III to the VI dynasty. The New Kingdom period (c.1550-1070 BC) saw an age of great military expansion, from Nubia in the south to the Euphrates River in the east.

MONUMENTAL BUILDINGS

The Egyptians built pyramids, huge funerary monuments, to house the bodies of their dead kings (pharaohs). The king was buried with precious goods to take on his journey into the afterlife. The Great Pyramid of Khufu (Cheops) at Giza (shown above) was built c.2551 BC. After about 2150 BC pyramids were no longer built and kings were buried in subterranean rock tombs.

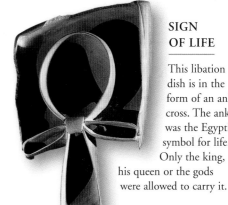

SIGN OF LIFE

This libation dish is in the form of an ankh cross. The ankh was the Egyptian symbol for life. Only the king, his queen or the gods were allowed to carry it.

THE FIRST WRITING

The first known system of writing appeared in Sumeria, north-east of Egypt, around 3200 BC, in the form of simple pictograms. The Egyptians developed this into an incredibly complex system of writing called hieroglyphs, using over 700 different symbols. The symbols expressed ideas rather than words and were used mostly for sacred writings.

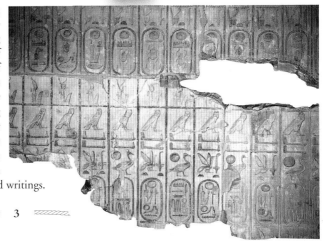

Life for the Rich

With the passage of over 6000 years it is very difficult for us today to obtain a complete picture about everyday life in ancient Egypt. As is the case for all societies at any period in the past, what remains are the belongings of the wealthy and, more especially, royalty. While the magnificent buildings, art and artefacts tell us a great deal about the sophistication and wealth of Egyptian society, they tell us very little about what life was like for ordinary people. Most of the hieroglyphs and scripts speak of government and ritual. Although much of our understanding of the lower orders of their society must remain speculative, at least we can be fairly certain that wealthier Egyptians and nobles enjoyed an opulent lifestyle. Comfort and hygiene featured strongly in their lives. They had strong family values and most wealthy households employed servants or slaves to carry out the mundane tasks.

ORNATE FURNITURE

Wood was in short supply in Egypt, but the wealthy could afford exotic imports, such as Lebanese cedar or ebony. Carpenters were skilled craftsmen and decorated their work with fine inlays and friezes, as seen in this chair.

ORNAMENTAL GLASS

The arts of glass-making and enamelling were well known to the Egyptians. They also made fine white and coloured porcelain of a comparable quality to that made in China. Houses of the wealthy were decorated with many fine art pieces, such as this beautiful glass perfume bottle in the shape of a bulti fish.

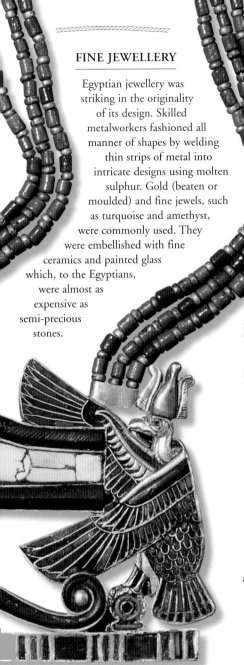

FINE JEWELLERY

Egyptian jewellery was striking in the originality of its design. Skilled metalworkers fashioned all manner of shapes by welding thin strips of metal into intricate designs using molten sulphur. Gold (beaten or moulded) and fine jewels, such as turquoise and amethyst, were commonly used. They were embellished with fine ceramics and painted glass which, to the Egyptians, were almost as expensive as semi-precious stones.

KEEPING UP APPEARANCES

Most Egyptians took a pride in their appearance, especially the wealthy who could afford the finest materials. Both men and women had their hair cut short, but wore elaborately braided and decorated wigs. The wealthier they were, the more elaborate their headdresses were, such as a gold headband decorated with semi-precious stones, as seen here. Both sexes seem also to have used cosmetics, in particular eye make-up.

SPACIOUS HOUSES

The houses of the rich were quite large, often occupying two stories, and were made from bricks covered in white painted plaster. They were raised on platforms as protection against damp as shown on this papyrus. Most also had a small, shady garden with an ornamental pool. Inside they were highly decorated with frescoes and enamelled wall paintings.

COMFORTABLE LIFESTYLE

Houses were quite comfortably, if simply, furnished, making great use of rare woods and fabrics imported from abroad. Most furniture was quite elaborately carved, such as lion-claw feet on tables and chairs. Beds, complete with stuffed mattresses, also had head and foot rests and reclining back boards. The wooden head rest shown here was probably used for resting during the day.

Life for the Poor

Over 90% of Egypt is desert. Virtually the only fertile region capable of supporting life, apart from small oases, was along the flood plains of the River Nile. This modern picture shows an almost timeless agricultural scene in Egypt. Many of the farming techniques practised today have hardly changed since ancient times.

Although life for the poor was hard in ancient Egypt, by comparison to other societies of the time, even they were comparatively well-off and had a reasonably high standard of living. Most peasants worked in the fields, while many others were employed in the massive building programmes of the pharaohs. Most were well treated. A stable family life was important to all classes of Egyptians. Great respect was accorded to elderly relatives. Once children became teenagers they often became servants to more affluent families. Houses, whether in town or country, were constructed of dried mud, mixed with straw and made into bricks. They were reasonably spacious, usually two stories, with flat roofs in which a vent was provided to catch the cool north winds.

GETTING ABOUT

Few poor people could afford wagons, horses or camels to transport themselves and their goods about. The most common form of transport for them was donkeys. There were few proper roads so transport was always difficult. For many people the only journeys they ever undertook were to and from the local market. Donkeys still provide the main means of transport for poor Egyptians in remote areas today.

BASIC ACCOMMODATION

This clay model shows a typical poor Egyptian's house with an arched doorway and small windows to keep the heat out. Known as a 'soul house', the model would have been buried with its owner to take into the next life.

A MEASURE OF WEALTH

The measure of a man's wealth was calculated by the number of beasts he owned, such as goats and geese, but particularly cattle. Scribes recorded the details and people were taxed accordingly. The agricultural season in ancient Egypt (as it still was until the construction of the Aswan dam in the 1960s) was governed by the annual flooding of the Nile. Each year the river burst its banks, depositing a thick black silt over a considerable distance of the surrounding land making it very fertile. Farmers also constructed irrigation channels from the river far into their fields to grow more crops inland.

HARD LABOUR

This wall painting from the Sennudem tomb in Thebes dates from *c*.1200 BC and shows farming practices at about that time. An ox is used to pull a rather primitive wooden plough. The ploughman is using a whip, made from papyrus, to swat flies and drive on the ox.

SLAVE TRADE

Although the ancient Egyptians did extend their rule over a small empire in north Africa and the eastern Mediterranean, they were not by nature a war-mongering people. When they did make forays into other lands, such as Nubia, Ethiopia or Lebanon, they captured native peoples and brought them back to Egypt as slaves. Some were put to work as servants in rich households, but mostly they provided the labour for the almost continuous building programmes of the pharaohs.

SPICE OF LIFE

Egypt was at the centre of the known world and all major trade routes passed through it, bringing exotic foods and spices from the East. Banquets could be exceptionally lavish with a variety of meats, fruit, vegetables, poultry and eggs.

VINTAGE WINE

The Egyptians grew grapes both as a table dessert and for making wine. Wine was usually only drunk by the rich. The more common alcoholic drink was beer, made from barley. It had a thick consistency and was drunk through a syphon.

A SWEETENER

To sweeten their foods, Egyptians generally used either fruits, such as dates mashed down, or honey. Bees were kept in conical pottery hives, as shown here. They were thought of as small birds rather than as insects.

FAMILY AFFAIR

This detail from a stucco wall painting comes from the tomb of Sennedjem and shows the tomb owner and his wife working in the fields. There was no centrally organized system of agriculture and each family produced its own food, taking any excess to market. The Egyptians are believed to have invented the first ox-drawn plough, about 3100 BC.

Food & Drink

Most Egyptians seem to have eaten very well, though they did suffer periodic plagues of insects (such as locusts) that destroyed crops and caused famine. Their agricultural methods were somewhat primitive (given the sophistication of their society as a whole) and most practised a subsistence form of farming, growing just sufficient for their needs. Nevertheless, the average Egyptian was able to choose from a wide variety of foods, including various meats, fish, vegetables (such as onions, leeks, turnips and garlic) and fruits (including grapes, figs, dates and pomegranates). They also perfected the technique of artificially incubating chickens to ensure plentiful supplies of poultry. Wine was a great favourite, particularly with the wealthy, and was made from both grapes and dates. During the 7th century AD, Egypt was overrun by Arabs, which changed many of the fundamental ways of life. Islam became the official religion and as Muslims are not allowed to drink alcohol the production of wine and beer went into decline.

THE BUTCHER'S TRADE

Wealthy Egyptians enjoyed a variety of meats, including sheep, oxen, poultry and wild animals, such as antelope, as shown here. Butchers often gave part of the slaughtered animals as religious sacrifices. Poorer people could not afford much meat and usually caught fish as a freely available substitute.

OPEN HEARTHS

Cooking was usually done in clay ovens or open charcoal fires, as shown here. The kitchen was often located outside, away from the living rooms, to avoid the risk of fires and reduce smells.

The boy in this wooden sculpture is fanning a fire in preparation to cook the duck in his hand.

ROUGHAGE

The Egyptian diet contained plenty of roughage as flour used in bread-making was only coarsely ground. Bread, made from barley and wheat, formed the staple diet of many Egyptians. Loaves were placed into flat round moulds. Bakers also made a variety of cakes using fruits such as figs or dates.

Pastimes

Most of the evidence so far gleaned about everyday life in ancient Egypt would seem to indicate that, certainly in its heyday around the time of the XVIII and XIX dynasties (*c.*1550-1196 BC) life was generally good for most people. They spent a high proportion of their time in the pursuit of leisure, which is normally indicative of a wealthy society. Those people from poorer societies are usually too preoccupied with the essentials of life, such as providing food and shelter. Not so, the Egyptians. Their society was refined and orderly, which is reflected in the nature of their pastimes. Many of them are family or solitary pursuits. They did not appear to engage in large-scale public entertainment, such as the theatre or stadiums, as did the Greeks and Romans.

ORIGIN OF THE OLYMPICS?

This relief of two young men boxing comes from the temple of Ramesses III. Egyptians were keen on active exercise to promote good health. Other popular sports were wrestling, gymnastics and jousting from boats, which may have inspired the Greek Olympics.

GYPSIES

Modern-day gypsies may not be descended from eastern Europeans, as is sometimes suggested, but from Egyptians who fled their homeland at the time of the Greek occupation. Many traditional gypsy pastimes, like horse racing and communal singing and dancing, may also have been practised in ancient Egypt.

EXOTIC DANCERS

A popular pastime in the king's palace, or at banquets held by the rich, was song and dance. Servant girls undertook rigorous dance training and they performed, sometimes naked, alongside gymnasts and jugglers, while musicians played. Dancing also often accompanied religious ceremonies.

THE FIRST HARP

It is believed that the Egyptians invented the harp (shown left) sometime around 3100 BC. Harps varied in size from small, lyre-like examples to ones taller than a man, the hollow chamber usually made out of wood. Other early instruments included the flute, made from hollow reeds, bronze cymbals, and tambourines.

SENET

This senet board is intricately made from wood and contains a drawer to house the playing pieces. The board is divided into 30 squares and dates from about 1200 BC.

BOARD GAMES

Board games were very popular with the Egyptians. The most popular was senet, in which two players tried to reach the kingdom of the gods. In the example left, the board has been drawn onto a papyrus sheet. Other games, more familiar today, were backgammon and chess. One of the oldest games ever discovered was 'snake', in which players moved pieces around a spiral board to the snake's head in the centre.

FAMILY VALUES

Egyptian society, at all levels, placed great store in family values. Families were quite large, with between 8 and 12 children. Though children were expected to work, there was still plenty of time for play. Egyptians were great storytellers and everyone gathered round to hear the father recite tales of the gods and of heroic exploits.

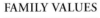

Fashion

All Egyptians liked to adorn their bodies with brightly painted cosmetics or jewellery, even the poorer classes, who simply used cheaper materials. Personal appearance and hygiene seem to have been very important to them and they were surprisingly fashion-conscious. Egypt was at the centre of most of the trade routes to the Mediterranean and the East and new materials brought back from countries such as India were quickly bought up. Because of the hot climate, most clothes were simple, light and loose fitting. Men usually wore only a kilt or even just a loin cloth. Women wore skirts or dresses, similar to Indian saris. Many women are known to have gone topless and nudity was common amongst children up to the age of 12.

HEADDRESS

It was fashionable for men and women to wear either wigs, made from human hair and held in place by beeswax, or headdresses. These might take the form of elaborate hats with stiffened collars made of fine material, or resemble wigs, with finely braided hair and decorated with jewels. For the poorer classes, working in the fierce Egyptian sun, skull caps or bonnets sufficed.

HAIRSTYLES

Most men and women had their hair cut short. They favoured the use of wigs, or hair extensions fastened with hair pins made of wood or bone. Finely toothed combs made of wood or, as shown here, ivory, were used to create elaborate hairstyles on the wigs.

FOOTWEAR

This picture shows the production of papyrus, used to make a wide range of objects, including shoes. Occasionally shoes were made of leather, but most footwear consisted of simple sandals made from papyrus reeds. They were cheap to make and easily replaced, favoured by people of all classes, including royalty and priests.

VÉRITABLE EXTRAIT DE VIANDE LIEBIG.

Histoire du papier. 2.
Fabricants de papier égyptiens.

BODY BEAUTIFUL

Cosmetics were widely used and held in elaborately carved containers, such as shown above. Various minerals (some poisonous) were ground up to form pastes. Green eye mascara, made from malachite, was a favourite amongst men and women.

ADORNMENTS

Poorer people wore jewellery, such as rings and bracelets made of cheap metals and decorated with pieces of brightly painted clay. The wealthy made great use of gold and precious stones, freely available from the East. Metalworkers became very skilled at making jewellery by fashioning strips of metal into elaborate shapes, or by casting. This gold and lapis lazuli necklace (left) and scarab pectoral (right) came from the tomb of Tutankhamun.

PLEATED DRESS

Women usually wore long, loose fitting dresses, often made out of one piece of material and pleated. The over-tunic shown here is believed to be the oldest surviving garment in the world and dates from about 3000 BC.

Art & Architecture

O ne of the most striking things about the remains of ancient Egypt is the monumental scale of its architecture. Whilst not in any way detracting from the skills of the masons responsible, not everything is as it first seems. Many of the huge monuments were not so much constructed as carved out of solid rock; an incredible feat in itself, of course, but one relating more perhaps to art than to architecture. The Sphinx at Giza, for example, was created in this way, as were many of the monolithic statues and entrance portals of the temples. Even the Great Pyramid contains an immense mound of natural bedrock at its core. We know much of everyday life in ancient Egypt from the engravings and reliefs etched into temple walls and pillars. The angular form of these carvings is very different from the huge statues, which were executed with perfect perspective; a remarkable achievement considering their great height. The Egyptians created many fine works of art, including wall paintings, statues, pottery and jewellery, but they saw them as intrinsic parts of life itself and not separate objects.

MONUMENTAL ART

Most of the more significant works of art and architecture to survive are from temples and tombs. Built on a grand scale, they are not representative of ancient Egyptian society as a whole. Monumental works on such a scale were never attempted again, not even in classical Greece and Rome. This view shows King Ramesses the Great at Luxor.

ARTISTIC LICENCE

Art was seen as an essential part of architecture, and indeed of life itself. It told a story and attempted to place everything in a natural order. Accompanying texts and hieroglyphs explained what the artist was trying to convey.

TEMPLE OF ABU SIMBEL

Ramesses II was something of an egoist and revived the colossal style of architectural building that had somewhat gone out of fashion amongst his predecessors. He constructed numerous huge statues of himself throughout Egypt. At Abu Simbel, in the Upper Nile, he built an impressive temple to himself and three gods (Amun, Re-Harakhty and Ptah). It is fronted by four huge statues of himself.

OBELISKS

Obelisks are tall, squared monoliths with pointed tops. They were usually placed in pairs at the entrance to temples. Hieroglyphs carved on their sides reflected who built them and to which deity they were dedicated. This one, along with the colossal statues of Ramesses II are to be seen at Luxor.

TEMPLE OF KARNAK

The Egyptians never mastered the use of arches. Instead, they roofed their immense buildings with huge flat slabs or corbelling, a series of slabs, each built out from the one below in decreasing steps until the gap was closed. This view shows the temple at Karnak, built by Ramesses II.

THE PYRAMIDS

The great pyramids of Giza were built as tombs for mighty Egyptian pharoahs. The Great Pyramid (right) was built around 2551 BC to house the body of King Khufu. His mummified body was entombed in a secret chamber to safeguard against grave robbers, along with treasures for him to take into the afterlife. Despite hidden entrances and blocked-off passageways, Khufu's tomb was still looted and the robber's tunnel is now the main entrance. Built with phenomenal precision, it stands some 146.6 metres (481 ft) high, contains about 2,300,000 blocks of stone, and the base is level to within 2.1cm (less than 1 inch).

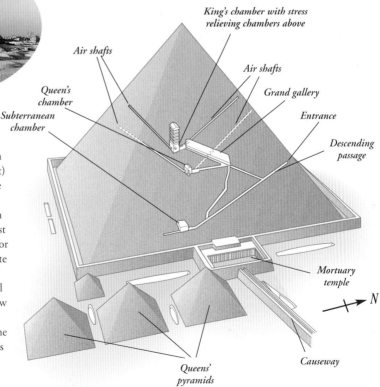

King's chamber with stress relieving chambers above

Air shafts

Air shafts

Grand gallery

Queen's chamber

Entrance

Subterranean chamber

Descending passage

Mortuary temple

N

Queens' pyramids

Causeway

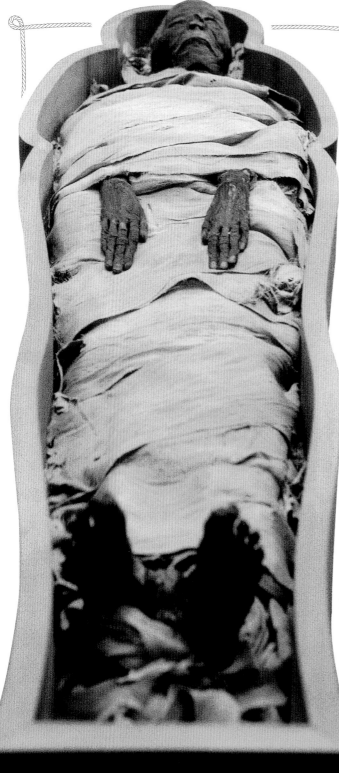

EMBALMING

Embalmers, although skilled in anatomy, were not doctors. They understood the causes of decay in bodies and so removed all of the internal organs, and pumped a bituminous substance into the body to preserve it for its journey into the afterlife. Incredibly, the brain was removed through the nostrils!

DOCTOR PRIESTS

In the early years of their civilization, the Egyptians saw disease as the result of an invasion of the body by evil spirits. Until physicians were allowed to practice medicine, only priests were permitted to cure the sick who would come to the temples such as this one at Edfou for treatment.

ANATOMY

Because Egyptians believed in an afterlife, doctors were forbidden to dissect human corpses. They had to rely on the dissection and examination of animals for their understanding of anatomy. They understood that the heart was the centre of the circulatory system and the various functions of the organs within the body, including the brain.

Health & Medicine

*T*he ancient Egyptians possessed considerable medical skills. Surviving texts also reveal that they had a surprisingly accurate knowledge of human anatomy. Nevertheless, medical treatment was a strange mixture of magic and science. Physicians and magicians often worked together to concoct potions to ward off evil spirits. Many ailments were thought to be caused by worm-like creatures that had to be purged from the body. Many of their herbal cures such as garlic, used in cooking and as a medicine, are still widely used today. Magical charms in the form of amulets were worn as protection against disease, and votive offerings or sacrifices were made to the gods. Because Egyptians believed in an afterlife, they did not believe ill-health was confined to the living so they buried magical charms with the deceased as protection in the underworld. Life expectancy was generally high and many Egyptians lived to age 80 and beyond.

DENTISTRY

This relief comes from the tomb of Hesire, chief dentist and physician to the king, and dates from *c.*2700 BC. Studies of mummified bodies have revealed quite sophisticated dentistry skills. Egyptian doctors were not general practitioners, but each specialised in a particular part of the body.

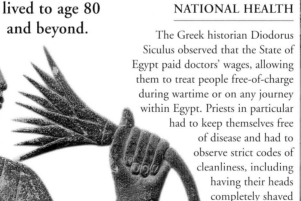

NATIONAL HEALTH

The Greek historian Diodorus Siculus observed that the State of Egypt paid doctors' wages, allowing them to treat people free-of-charge during wartime or on any journey within Egypt. Priests in particular had to keep themselves free of disease and had to observe strict codes of cleanliness, including having their heads completely shaved as shown here.

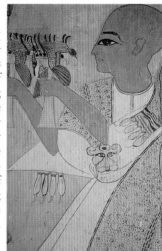

PURE AIR

Breathing the scent of the sacred lotus flower was thought to be a protection against disease. Egyptians knew of the healing properties of several plants, such as hemlock and opium, which they made into ointments and gargles.

Love & Marriage

There is some evidence to suggest that incestuous relationships between brother and sister were sometimes allowed in ancient Egypt, usually amongst royalty. In religion, the sky goddess Nut was married to her brother, the earth god Geb, seen here.

Ordinary people in Egyptian society lived a comparatively relaxed lifestyle in which there was much time for enjoyment and socializing. After about the age of 12, children were regarded as young adults and could marry; especially girls, whose career prospects were more limited than boys. After marriage, men's obligations were to provide for their own family; the responsibility of looking after elderly parents fell to the women. Although priests were expected to devote their lives to the gods and carry out their duties on behalf of the pharaoh, they occupied a very high place in the social hierarchy and were allowed to marry and have families. They benefited from a very privileged form of inheritance which allowed them to acquire vast riches and land, which they held collectively as a priesthood. Priests' sons were allowed to inherit this great wealth and enjoyed a very exalted position in society.

GODDESS OF FERTILITY

The Egyptian goddess of fertility was Taweret, usually shown as a pregnant hippopotamus. Taweret is often depicted with a fierce countenance to ward off evil during childbirth. Women said prayers and made votive offerings to her during their pregnancy. In general, however, hippos were normally regarded as evil, especially the males, which were seen as the enemies of the gods Osiris and Horus.

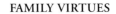

FAMILY VIRTUES

By all accounts ancient Egyptians were a gentle race who observed many social graces. Single girls of high rank were chaperoned on their meetings with men and many marriages were arranged between both sets of parents to facilitate a better match, or to secure an income or inheritance. This was especially true for women, who seldom had an income of their own.

GIRL POWER

Ancient Egypt was very much a patriarchial society, though women married to important nobles could exert a great deal of influence behind the scenes. Sometimes wives at court would gather together, under the protection of the goddess Hathar, and petition their husbands. This devoted couple probably remained married throughout their lives, as was normal in high society; the heavy wigs denote their wealth. Women did not give up their acquired status easily.

DEVOTED COUPLE

Unlike other Middle-Eastern societies, ancient Egyptians were largely monogamous (men were only allowed one wife at a time) though some of the pharaohs and nobles may have had more. Apparently, it was very easy for people of all classes to obtain an annulment of their marriage. This *stela* (a kind of religious inscription placed inside a tomb, like a gravestone) shows a devoted couple who share the same grave and presumably hoped to travel to the afterlife together.

WEDDING CEREMONY

This wall painting shows a Nubian called Sennufer marrying his bride. They are being blessed with holy water by the high priest, using a sacred container called a *situla*. Brides often wore sacred lotus blossoms in their hair for good luck, or delicately perfumed pomanders fastened to their brocaded wigs.

Women & Children

Although ancient Egyptian society was dominated by men (few positions of power or authority were given to women), women nevertheless played an important role in providing a stable family environment. Only the wealthy could afford servants or slaves to perform menial tasks. For most families the responsibility of looking after the house, caring for the children, cooking and cleaning rested with the women. There were few professions open to women. Most doctors and priests were men, though occasionally a woman of high rank might become a priestess. However, male dominance was more by custom than by law.

CHILDREN'S GAMES

These carvings show children carrying models in the shape of birds. These would have been floated on water in much the same way as model boats are used today. Many modern games can be traced back to Egyptian times, including leap frog, piggy-back and tug-of-war.

CLEOPATRA

Egypt was overrun by invaders several times from about 1000 BC on, including by the Greeks, under Alexander the Great. Cleopatra VII (shown left), although of Greek descent, was the last in the long line of rulers of Egypt. Unusually for a woman, she ruled in her own right. She embarked on a disastrous love-affair with the Roman general, Anthony, and together they challenged the might of Rome. When their combined armies were defeated by Octavius in AD 30, Cleopatra committed suicide. From then on, Egypt became a mere Roman province, ruled over by the Emperors.

TIME-HONOURED TRADITION

Two of the principal roles for women were to make and wash the clothes for the family. The most common material was linen, woven from the stems of the flax plant, making a strong and durable fabric. The first loom appeared in Egypt around 3000 BC.

QUEEN NEFERTITI

Women rarely ruled in their own right in ancient Egypt, although there are a few notable exceptions. Queen Nefertiti, who ruled with her husband Akhenaten, was much hated and after their deaths both their names were removed from many books and inscriptions. She aided Akhenaten in banishing the worship of all the old gods, including Amun-Re, in favour of Aten, a sun god. Around 1333 BC, Tutankhamun restored the old gods to prominence.

HARVESTING

Much of the agricultural work was performed by women and children. The woman shown here is picking fruit whilst carrying her child in a kind of papoose.

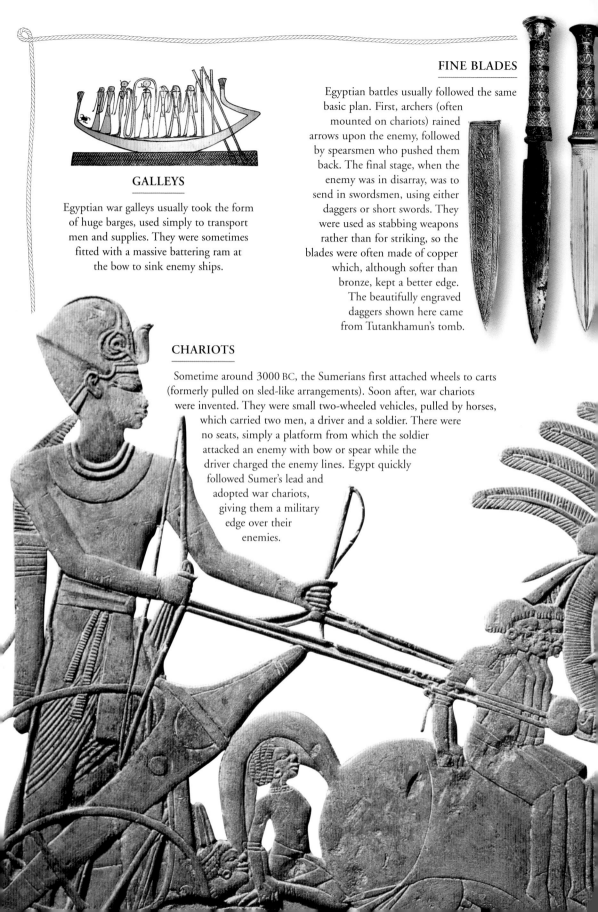

GALLEYS

Egyptian war galleys usually took the form of huge barges, used simply to transport men and supplies. They were sometimes fitted with a massive battering ram at the bow to sink enemy ships.

FINE BLADES

Egyptian battles usually followed the same basic plan. First, archers (often mounted on chariots) rained arrows upon the enemy, followed by spearsmen who pushed them back. The final stage, when the enemy was in disarray, was to send in swordsmen, using either daggers or short swords. They were used as stabbing weapons rather than for striking, so the blades were often made of copper which, although softer than bronze, kept a better edge. The beautifully engraved daggers shown here came from Tutankhamun's tomb.

CHARIOTS

Sometime around 3000 BC, the Sumerians first attached wheels to carts (formerly pulled on sled-like arrangements). Soon after, war chariots were invented. They were small two-wheeled vehicles, pulled by horses, which carried two men, a driver and a soldier. There were no seats, simply a platform from which the soldier attacked an enemy with bow or spear while the driver charged the enemy lines. Egypt quickly followed Sumer's lead and adopted war chariots, giving them a military edge over their enemies.

War & Weaponry

rom about 5000-3100 BC two separate kingdoms flourished; Upper and Lower Egypt. In about 3100 BC, King Menes united the two kingdoms and founded the I dynasty. Egyptian civilization flourished after that date, but settlements were mostly centred in the Nile valley itself. During what is known as the New Kingdom period (c.1550-1070 BC), Egypt expanded its domains to form a small empire, stretching from Nubia in the south to Sumer and Syria in the north. Although generally not a war-like nation, in order to protect its borders Egypt adapted an aggressive stance towards its neighbours. Egypt was a rich country and often attracted the greedy attentions of other nations, so much of the efforts of its army were concentrated on protecting itself. Later Egypt was subjected to wave after wave of invasion, when the greatness of their earlier civilization fell and it became a mere province of first the Persians and then the Greeks, Romans and Arabs, who supplanted Egyptian culture with their own.

TACTICS

The army was a highly organized and well-disciplined fighting machine. The usual tactics were for the soldiers to march in divisions of about 50 straight towards the enemy lines and overcome them by sheer weight of numbers.

The pharaoh usually participated in military campaigns. Ramesses II is seen here overcoming his enemies, the Nubians, Libyans and Syrians.

WARRIORS

The favoured weapons in the Egyptian army were the spear and the battle-axe. Axes were often quite elaborate, with bronze heads. Soldiers had comparatively light armour, usually helmets and large wooden shields, used as protection against arrows or the thrusting spear of an enemy soldier.

PROTECTION OF THE GODS

When the Egyptians undertook a military campaign, they invoked the power of the gods to both protect and assist them in striking down their enemies. Wars were fought with great pomp and ceremony, with trumpeters to accompany the army. A mast was carried on the pharaoh's chariot, decorated with a ram's head and a symbol of the sun to represent Amun-Re. Many other gods might accompany the army, including Khansu the moon god, shown here.

Crime & Punishment

Egyptian society demanded strict codes of law that everyone was expected to follow. By modern standards, some of these laws might seem harsh, but most pharaohs worked on the assumption that if the citizens were properly protected against crime then they would not only be more content but would give more back to society itself. Some laws were introduced to promote better hygiene, such as compulsory circumcision. It was everyone's duty to prevent or report crimes, or to go to someone's aid if they were in danger. To not do so was in itself a crime. Crimes against women were punished by mutilation: adulterous women were made ugly by having their noses amputated, whilst pregnant women who had committed a crime were only punished after they had given birth. Similarly, forgers had their hands cut off and those guilty of treason had their tongues removed. A soldier guilty of any crime had to make amends by performing a heroic deed.

COUNTERFEIT

A coined monetary system was not introduced into Egypt until 525 BC when the Persians invaded. After that date anyone found guilty of making counterfeit coins had their hands cut off. The gold coin shown here is of Cleopatra's time (c.AD 40).

ALL-SEEING GOD

The pharaoh was thought to be the embodiment of the hawk-headed sky god Horus. He was an all-seeing god who ensured that every citizen was protected. If a guilty person escaped accusation and punishment in life, they might still pay the price in death. If they were justly accused of a crime, even after death, they might be denied burial honours and so be robbed of the opportunity to enter the afterlife.

SLAVE TRADE

This relief from the temple of Ramesses III shows defeated Philistines being led into captivity with a rope tied around their necks. Egyptian society made great use of slaves captured from defeated countries, particularly in the years of the New Kingdom, after 1550 BC. Slaves provided much of the labour for the massive building programmes of the pharaohs and many died in the process.

CITIZEN'S DUTY

Egyptian society was largely self-policing. It was the duty of every citizen to prevent crimes or to follow up with their punishment. Everyone had the right to accuse and prosecute a criminal. If witnesses did not fulfil their duty they were beaten with branches.

LAW OF DECLARATION

Each year every individual had to provide a written report to the magistrate of the province in which they lived stating how they made their legal means of existence, whether as bakers as shown above, herdsmen or scribes. If they did not, it was assumed they did so illegally and were executed.

HONOUR AMONG THIEVES

Among other things, Thoth was the god of wisdom and truth. He had the ability to know the evils that lay in men's hearts and is seen here, in baboon form, apprehending a thief. Strangely, thieves could register their profession and declare their earnings to an official, but if a victim of theft could accurately describe his possessions, he could claim 75% of his goods back; the remaining 25% remained the property of the thief.

Transport & Science

The ancient Egyptians were responsible for introducing or developing many new ideas. Several, such as the potter's wheel, are still in use today. Although it is now believed that Egypt (and indeed the whole of north Africa) was less arid than it is today, natural materials such as wood were never in abundance. However, stone and papyrus were, and the Egyptians were very resourceful in making maximum use of these commodities. Papyrus is a triangular-stemmed reed that grows to a height of about 3 metres (13 ft). All parts of the plant were used and so extensively that it almost disappeared completely, although it has now been re-introduced into Egypt. As most of the main centres of population were scattered down the length of the Nile, most long-distance journeys were made by boat. Egyptian boats were not particularly seaworthy and were used mostly on the calmer waters of the Nile itself.

PALANQUIN

The king and other important dignitaries were transported in a chariot or a decorated carriage for long journeys. For short journeys around the city, they would be carried in a palanquin, which was a canopied chair carried on two poles by four servants.

TIME IMMEMORIAL

Egyptian priests were also astronomers. By studying the movements of heavenly bodies they were able to accurately predict various natural phenomena, which they used in religious ceremonies. They devised an annual calendar of 365 days, divided into 12 equal months of 30 days, followed by five 'complementary' days.

WHEELED VEHICLES

About 3000 BC the Sumerians are believed to have created the first wheeled vehicle. The idea was soon copied and developed by the Egyptians, who made many more sophisticated vehicles, though none survive. (This is a later example from 9th century AD.)

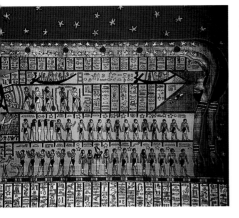

THE SKY GOD

The Egyptians studied the heavens in great detail and formed a fairly acceptable theory as to the origins of the universe. They saw the primeval chaos of the universe as water (Nun). The sun god Atum emerged from the sea as land (as Egypt itself did from the annual flood). From this were produced air (Shu), moisture (Tefnut), earth (Geb) and sky (Nut). Nut visited her earth husband daily by descending from the heavens and creating night. Eclipses were explained by Nut supposedly stealing away to visit Geb during the day.

REED BOATS

Many of the boats used in ancient Egypt were not made of wood, which was expensive and difficult to obtain, but of the much more readily available papyrus. The reeds were tightly bundled and then strapped to a frame, in a similar manner to roof thatching. They were made waterproof by lashing several layers together, which could be easily replaced if they became rotten or damaged. Propelled by oars, most fishermen used this kind of vessel.

WRITING IT ALL DOWN

Flat strips of papyrus were used in layers to form a very smooth and durable paper, usually cut into lengths and rolled into scrolls. Even the pens used to write with were made from papyrus stems.

RIVER TRANSPORT

This model, found in a tomb, is probably typical of many of the boats that plied the Nile. It was propelled by oars and a small sail and steered with a large oar at the stern, like a rudder.

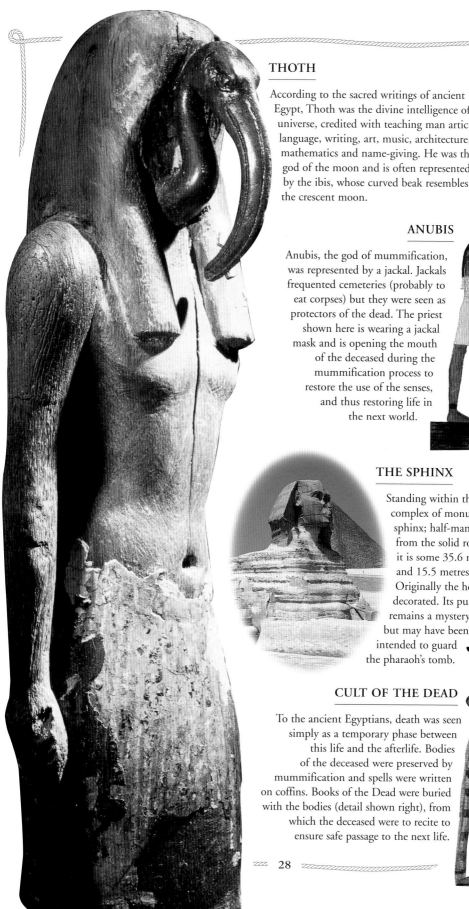

THOTH

According to the sacred writings of ancient Egypt, Thoth was the divine intelligence of the universe, credited with teaching man articulate language, writing, art, music, architecture, mathematics and name-giving. He was the god of the moon and is often represented by the ibis, whose curved beak resembles the crescent moon.

ANUBIS

Anubis, the god of mummification, was represented by a jackal. Jackals frequented cemeteries (probably to eat corpses) but they were seen as protectors of the dead. The priest shown here is wearing a jackal mask and is opening the mouth of the deceased during the mummification process to restore the use of the senses, and thus restoring life in the next world.

THE SPHINX

Standing within the extraordinary complex of monuments at Giza is a sphinx; half-man, half-lion. Carved from the solid rock in about 2500 BC it is some 35.6 metres (117 ft) long and 15.5 metres (51 ft) high. Originally the head was lavishly decorated. Its purpose remains a mystery, but may have been intended to guard the pharaoh's tomb.

CULT OF THE DEAD

To the ancient Egyptians, death was seen simply as a temporary phase between this life and the afterlife. Bodies of the deceased were preserved by mummification and spells were written on coffins. Books of the Dead were buried with the bodies (detail shown right), from which the deceased were to recite to ensure safe passage to the next life.

THE TEMPLE OF KARNAK

The magnificent temple at Karnak was begun between 1504-1592 BC. The columns and walls are decorated with lotus and papyrus carvings, two of the most enduring ancient Egyptian symbols. The temple, like many others, was dedicated to Amun-Re, protector of the pharaohs. Amun-Re is an amalgam of Amun (which means 'hidden') and Re (the sun god). He was perceived as the 'great primordial being'; the 'one true god'.

*T*here were several hundred different gods and goddesses in ancient Egypt, many of whom manifested themselves as animals on earth. When priests carried out their rituals they would often wear the appropriate animal mask so as to give the impression to the largely uneducated masses that they were the actual god. It is not easy to unravel the complexities of the Egyptian gods, especially as the same animal might represent several different gods in different regions. However, the one 'true god', and king of all the other gods, was Amun-Re, the sun god. The ancient Egyptians kept many libraries of books, mostly of sacred writings, and many talk of a belief in an afterlife. They believed in an underworld, called Duat, where the dead had to make a perilous journey to reach a kind of 'promised land'. To aid them in their journey, bodies were mummified (or preserved) and they were given magic spells to ward off the evils they would encounter.

THE SACRED TRIAD

Amun-Re was perceived as a triad of divinities, Amun (the father), Mouth (the mother) and Khons (the son). They manifested themselves on earth as Osiris, Isis and Horus, respectively.

ISIS

This picture shows the goddess Isis, suckling her infant son, Horus. Isis and Osiris were instructed by Thoth to civilize the human race and lead them away from the ways of animals. Isis was a fertility goddess, associated with mother Earth and the cycle of birth, death and re-birth in the afterlife. Her shrines in temples were often tended by women. The Romans adopted her into their own religion following their conquest of Egypt.

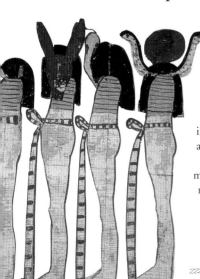

Legacy of the Past

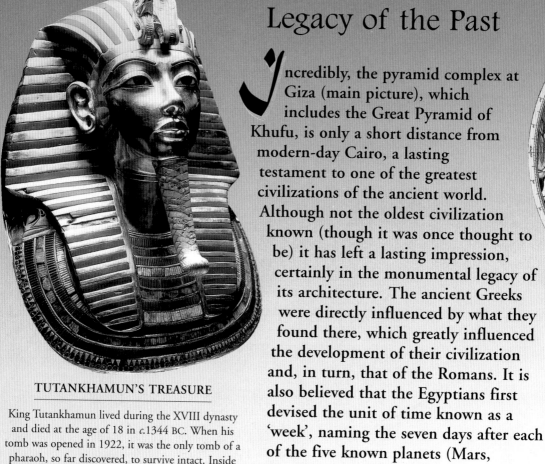

Incredibly, the pyramid complex at Giza (main picture), which includes the Great Pyramid of Khufu, is only a short distance from modern-day Cairo, a lasting testament to one of the greatest civilizations of the ancient world. Although not the oldest civilization known (though it was once thought to be) it has left a lasting impression, certainly in the monumental legacy of its architecture. The ancient Greeks were directly influenced by what they found there, which greatly influenced the development of their civilization and, in turn, that of the Romans. It is also believed that the Egyptians first devised the unit of time known as a 'week', naming the seven days after each of the five known planets (Mars, Mercury, Jupiter, Venus and Saturn), the sun and the moon.

TUTANKHAMUN'S TREASURE

King Tutankhamun lived during the XVIII dynasty and died at the age of 18 in *c.*1344 BC. When his tomb was opened in 1922, it was the only tomb of a pharaoh, so far discovered, to survive intact. Inside was an astonishing array of jewellery, artefacts and decorative art, unsurpassed in the ancient world. His magnificent funerary face mask, shown above, was made of gold, inlaid with blue lapis lazuli. Treasures from the tomb have been displayed around the world and always generate a great deal of interest. The exhibition in Cairo Museum is now a major tourist attraction in its own right.

WRITTEN IN THE STARS

It was the astronomer priests of ancient Egypt who, around 2500 BC, first devised the zodiac, still in use today. In those days astrology and astronomy were seen as the same thing and given a great deal of scientific credibility. By observing the heavens over many centuries and carefully recording their findings, Egyptian astronomers divided the skies into 12 constellations, each closely representing a particular aspect of their beliefs.

architrave *capital*

UNIQUE ARCHITECTURE

Egyptian architecture displays many characteristics that are unique and set it apart from European styles of building. The closest parallels are to be seen in the Aztec and Inca buildings of South and Central America (coincidentally, also pyramid builders of a later age). The most striking features are the irregularly shaped and incredibly accurate masonry joints, and the columns, which have square blocks on top of the capitals to support the architrave above.

THE POTTER'S WHEEL

Of all the tchnological achievements handed down to us by the ancient Egyptians, perhaps the most enduring is the potter's wheel. Invented around 4000 BC it changed the face of civilization for all time, enabling elaborate pieces to be mass-produced for the first time. Operated by a simple treadle mechanism, the basic design has hardly changed at all.

DID YOU KNOW?

That the Egyptians first used aromatherapy?
Many so-called 'alternative' medicines have their origins in the distant past. Aromatherapy, for instance, was first used by the ancient Egyptians to cure many stress-related, respiratory and muscular ailments. Powerful aromas, extracted from plants, were used to alter the patient's state of mind and so allow the gods to cure them. Modern doctors are now beginning to appreciate the benefits of such treatments.

That the Egyptians may have invented zero in mathematics? Mathematicians often debate the virtues of zero as a number, or whether, in fact, it is a number at all. It behaves differently to other numbers: it is not used in counting; if multiplied by any other number, the answer is always zero; if added to the right of any number, that number increases tenfold. The Egyptians first recognised the need to express zero in mathematics when making up the royal accounts and it was necessary to show the answer when subtracting two equal amounts from one another.

That the Egyptians were the first to study astronomy? Mankind has always observed natural phenomena such as the seasons, and governed his life accordingly. By using their knowledge of mathematics, however, the ancient Egyptians discovered that certain events like eclipses were repeated on a regular basis so could be predicted with astonishing accuracy and used for religious rituals. They also observed that Sirius, the dog star, appeared at a precise location immediately prior to the annual flooding of the Nile, which the priests used in their fertility ceremonies.

That the tombs of the pharaohs were protected by a curse? In order to protect the dead pharaohs and their possessions in their journey to the afterlife, their tombs were protected by a curse that said anyone who defiled their tombs would die. Coincidentally, following the discovery of Tutankhamun's tomb in 1922, several of those involved died violent deaths, including Lord Carnarvon, financier of the expedition, who died from an infected mosquito bite five months later. However, modern archaeologists have detected traces of poisons painted onto the walls of tombs which may have aided the curse to come true!

That the temples of Abu Simbel were rebuilt in modern times? In the 1960s it was decided to build a massive dam on the Nile at Aswan to relieve Egypt's water shortages. Unfortunately, several important archaeological sites would have been lost in the process, including the temples of Queen Nefertari and Ramesses II at Abu Simbel. An international rescue bid was mounted, at a cost of over £16 million, and the huge temples and statues were carefully dismantled, the pieces numbered and then carefully reconstructed 230 metres further up the rock face, safely above the water line.

ACKNOWLEDGEMENTS

We would like to thank: Graham Rich and Elizabeth Wiggans for their assistance and David Hobbs for his map of the world.
Copyright © 2004 *ticktock* **Entertainment Ltd,** Unit 2, Orchard Business Centre, North Farm Road, Tunbridge Wells, Kent TN2 3XF, U.K. First published in Great Britain 1998. All rights reserved.
No part of this publication may be reproduced, stored in a retrieval system, or transmitted in any form or by any means electronic, mechanical, photocopying, recording or otherwise, without prior written permission of the copyright owner.
A CIP catalogue record for this book is available from the British Library. ISBN 1 86007 577 0
Picture research by Image Select. Printed in China.
The most up-to-date spellings have been used, rather than the sometimes more familiar spellings

Picture Credits:
t=top, b=bottom, c=centre, l=left, r=right, OFC=outside front cover, IFC=inside front cover, OBC=outside back cover, IBC=inside back cover

AKG; 27tr. Ancient Art and Architecture; OFC (main pic), 4tl, 10br & OFC, 11tr, 17br, 19br, 21br, 20/21ct, 22tr, 23br, 24tl, 30tl & OFC. Ann Ronan at Image Select; 7r, 8t, 8c, 13tr, 15c, 16l, 18/19c. Chris Fairclough Colour Library /Image Select; 2/3ct, 6bl, 14/15ct, 16cr. et archive; 7bl, 10/11c, 16/17ct, 22b & OBC, 28/29cb. Giraudon; 29tr. Image Select; 10bl, 13bl, 14tl, 21c & 32c, 27cr, 28c. National Maritime Museum, London; 31tl. PIX; 2bl, 3cl, 6/7c & OBC, 15tr, 15cl & OFC, 20tl, 20bl, 22tl, 23cb, 24bl, 28/29cb, 31tr. Spectrum Colour Library; 20br, 27br, 31l, 30/31(main pic). Werner Forman Archive; 2tr, 3cr, 3br, 4bl, 5br, 5tr, 5c, 4/5c, 7tr, 8l & OFC, 8bl, 9tr, 9br, 8/9c, 10tl, 10/11ct, 11br, 12br, 12l, 13br, 13c & OBC, 13cr & OFC, 14bl, 16/17cb, 17tr, 18tl, 18bl & OBC, 19c, 19tr, 23tr, 24/25c, 25t, 25br, 26tl, 26bl, 26/27c, 28l, 28r.

Every effort has been made to trace the copyright holders and we apologize in advance for any unintentional omissions.
We would be pleased to insert the appropriate acknowledgement in any subsequent edition of this publication.